Wha
What's That?

Written by Jane Sikic
Illustrated by Bettina Guthridge

™
sundance
A Haights Cross Communications Company

What's this? What's that?

a cat on a mat

What's this? What's that?

a frog on a log

What's this? What's that?

a rat in a hat

What's this? What's that?

a mouse in a house

What's this? What's that?

a bear in a chair